TM

Mothers Meeting to Pray for Their Children & Schools

by Fern Nichols

Moms In Touch International
P.O. Box 1120
Poway, California 92074-1120
U.S.A.

Phone: 858-486-4065
e-mail: info@MomsInTouch.org
www.MomsInTouch.org

Table of Contents

Introduction

n the fall of 1984, the two oldest of our four children were entering junior high school. I found myself with a heart heavy and burdened with concern for the new world they would be entering. They would be facing their greatest test in resisting immoral values, vulgar language and peer pressure. My heart cried out to the Lord asking Him to protect them, enable them to see clearly the difference between right and wrong, and to make good decisions.

The burden to intercede for my boys was so overwhelming that I knew I could not bear it alone. I asked God to give me another mom who felt the same burden and who would be willing to pray with me concerning our children and their schools. God heard the cry of my heart and led me to phone another mom who voiced her agreement as I shared my burden. We also thought of a few other moms we believed would want to pray. We called them and began meeting the following week for prayer.

This was the beginning of what is now known as Moms In Touch International—moms in touch with God, their children, their school, and one another through prayer. As moms began sharing what God had been doing in their lives, and in the lives of their children because of prayer, other groups began to spring up all over British Columbia where we were living at the time. There were groups formed from the elementary through the high school levels. The initial material in this booklet was formulated during that year. What a thrill to see God's plan unfold!

The summer of 1985 brought a change to our family as we moved from Abbotsford, British Columbia to Poway, California. I soon discovered that God had given me still greater opportunities for carrying on the work that began in Canada. I prayed that God would raisOe up moms who were willing to "stand in the gap" for their children.

God has been faithful to send moms who would pray. There are now Moms In Touch International groups across America, as well as in other countries. Because moms were asking for guidelines on how to pray more effectively and how to begin a Moms In Touch group, we created this booklet.

I would like to acknowledge Sondra Ball, who has helped me put together this material. Her encouragement, suggestions, time, friendship, and loving support have been specific answers to my prayers.

It is my hope that God will raise up moms to intercede for every school across our nation and around the world. What a thrilling thought to consider two or more moms gathered together every week in prayer for their children and their schools.

Let me challenge you to be involved in your child's life through prayer. See what God can do for your children and their schools when you are faithful to pray on a regular basis.

Believing in the power of prayer,

Fern Nichols

Fern Nichols

MILLER

Personal Testimony

I would like to take a moment to share with you how God has worked in my personal life on the matter of prayer. Being asked to speak at a prayer retreat brought about some serious evaluation of my prayer life. Listening to several tapes on prayer by Ron Dunn helped me greatly. I also read many wonderful books on prayer, but I knew within my heart that listening to discussions about prayer, talking about prayer, or reading about prayer didn't make up for my lack of actually praying.

It seemed I was always praying "on the run." My prayer time was hit and miss. God, in His grace, allowed me to see that my priorities were not right. I was "busy," productive in many wonderful things, but I wasn't doing the best thing—spending consistent prayer time with God.

I believe that Satan has us thinking that being spiritual means being productive. He doesn't want us to cross over the invisible line into powerful intercessory prayer. If he can keep us thinking that being on the productive side of the line is doing great things for God, then we will secure few blessings for our family, schools, community, and nation. But if we recognize the line and cross over it to be intercessors, God will move heaven and earth to answer our prayers, and we will begin to see great victories and Satan's defeat. Satan trembles when he sees the weakest saint on her knees, for he knows he has no power against our prayers. Let me share with you a list of what I asked God to do in my life in this matter of prayer.

1. That I would be a woman of prayer
2. That I would gain a vision for the power of prayer
3. That I would seek to become an intercessor

4. That I would begin to practice aggressive praying, taking the initiative to pray with others as a way of life
5. That I would learn to pray through the Scriptures
6. That I might pray without ceasing
7. That I would be able to communicate to others what God is teaching me in prayer

If the Holy Spirit is speaking to your heart as you read this list, stop right now, heed His voice, and pray.

I believe the ministry of prayer is the highest calling a Christian can have. Right now, Jesus is seated at the right hand of God interceding for you.

What is Moms In Touch?

- Two or more moms who meet for one hour a week to release God's power on their children and schools through prayer.
- Mothers, grandmothers, or any woman who is willing to pray for a specific child and school.
- Moms who believe that prayer makes a difference!

"Pour out your heart like water before the face of the Lord, lift up your hands toward Him for the lives of your children."

Lamentations 2:19

Moms In Touch International is not a lobbying group, regardless of how worthy the cause. Participation in outside political and social issues must be done solely on an individual basis. Under no circumstances should the Moms In Touch International name be used in conjunction with outside issues.

Purpose

- To stand in the gap for our children through prayer
- To pray that our children will receive Jesus as Lord and Savior, then stand boldly in their faith
- To pray for teachers and staff
- To pray that teachers, administrative staff, and students would come to faith in Jesus Christ
- To pray that our schools may be directed by biblical values and high moral standards
- To be an encouragement and a positive support to our schools
- To provide support and encouragement to moms who carry heavy burdens for their children

Before You Start

- Pray that God brings you another mom from your child's school who will be willing to meet with you each week for prayer.
- Make a list of prospective moms from your school and ask them to join your prayer time.
- Read and agree with the Moms In Touch International Statement of Faith.
- Agree with the Moms In Touch International (MITI) policies, guidelines and the format for prayer time.
- Trust God for answers to prayer, focus on Him, and expect great things to happen. Make sure you are led by the Holy Spirit.

Starting a Group

As you begin:
1. Come as you are.
2. Be faithful in meeting for one hour on a weekly basis. Make this hour a solid commitment.
3. Start and finish on time.
4. Do not serve refreshments.
5. This prayer time is precious and should be undisturbed. We suggest placing a "Please Do Not Disturb" note on the door and disconnecting the phone.

Each mom needs:
1. A Bible and notebook for keeping Member Sheets (see sample on page 37)
2. Her own Moms In Touch International booklet
3. To allow another person the privilege of caring for her preschool children during this hour

In matters of prayer:
1. Pray conversationally in one accord using the four steps of prayer.
2. Do not get sidetracked in talking about your requests more than you are praying about them. Share your requests in prayer rather than discussing them first.
3. **Everything that is said or prayed about in a Moms In Touch meeting is confidential.** Nothing said should ever be shared with anyone outside of that Moms In Touch group. Confidentiality cannot be overemphasized.

For the leader*:

1. Leaders, please register your group online at our website, www.MomsInTouch.org or by filling out and returning the registration envelope in the center of this booklet. This will enable us to refer interested moms to your group as well as send you the Moms In Touch International newsletter. Your members may also receive the MITI newsletter by signing up on the website.

2. Re-read the Moms In Touch booklet periodically.

3. Pray about everything you do concerning MITI.

4. Each Moms In Touch group should represent only **one** school. This enables you to pray specifically for the needs of that school.

5. Moms with more than one child at a school are encouraged to focus on **one child** each week. This allows for more concentrated and specific prayer for that child during the given time for intercession.

6. For several meetings at the beginning of each school year, you will find it helpful to your group if you spend the first few minutes going over the information on praying in one accord.

7. Follow this format during your prayer hour: praise, confession, thanksgiving, and intercession.

8. MITI groups are **not** to meet on public school campuses nor impose upon the public school by asking for prayer requests and/or promotion of the ministry.

9. Once a group is started, it is important to maintain that group for the next school year. As a leader, you should seek to replace yourself if you find you will not be able to continue. It is good to allow another person to lead the group from time to time. This gives you the opportunity to train another person so that the group is not entirely dependent upon you.

10. You may want to consider meeting monthly during the summer break.

* More information is available in the MITI Leader's Guide.

Praying in One Accord

Method of Prayer

onversationally praying in one accord is the method of prayer that is used in our MITI groups. One accord praying is agreeing together as directed by the Holy Spirit. When a group prays in one accord, they concentrate on **one subject at a time.** More than one mom can pray on each subject until that subject is thoroughly covered. It is important not to start a new subject until every aspect of the subject you are praying about is covered. The leader guides the prayer meeting.

Do not be concerned about silence; God speaks during these times, too. Try to keep prayers **short** and **simple.** This will encourage everyone to participate.

"When people start praying together in one accord, to our Father in heaven, in the name of Jesus, and practice praying together, things begin to change. Our lives change, our families change, our school, church and communities change. Changes take place not when we study about prayer, not when we talk about it, not even when we memorize beautiful scripture verses on prayer. It is when we actually pray that things begin to happen."*

If you have never prayed conversationally before, please do not feel forced into praying aloud. If you pray silently in your heart, you are still praying in one accord. The more you experience conversational prayer, the easier it will be for you to eventually join in.

By praying in one accord, we hear the heartfelt thoughts of others, and echo those words in our hearts as well. This will cause us to focus on Almighty God and not on ourselves. He will give you the words to say. The eloquence of your prayer is not what is important. **The sincerity of your heart is what God hears.**

*Evelyn Christenson, *What Happens When Women Pray*

Prayer Time

Format: Four Steps of Prayer

Praise. Every Moms In Touch prayer session should begin with praise using the Word of God. Our faith becomes strong as we pray back to God His very words.

Let's illustrate the method of praising God in one accord. Choose a verse(s) Psalm 23:1 (NIV) for example, and read it aloud. *"The Lord is my shepherd, I shall not be in want."*

The group leader might begin by praying, "Oh Lord, I praise You that because You are my shepherd, I have everything I need. There is nothing I need You can't provide."

Another mom might continue by praying, "Father, I praise You that as a shepherd knows his sheep, You know exactly what my needs are."

A third mom might pray, "And, Lord, because You know my needs and You are God, I can trust You to give me what is best for me."

Additional prayer on God as the shepherd should continue until the subject is thoroughly covered.

As We Praise God:
1. It gives Him the glory.
2. It is declaring, proclaiming, confessing who God is.
3. It is for our good. It brings freedom and encouragement to our lives because we focus on God and not on the situation.
4. It leads to true stability in life and develops a gentle and quiet spirit.
5. It dispels Satan's power and he leaves. Psalm 22:3, *"God inhabits (resides, dwells in) the praises of His people."*

Here are some suggested Scriptures to use for your praise time.

Psalm 28:7	Psalm 103:8
Psalm 103:11	Psalm 145:9
I Chronicles 29:10-11	Psalm 33:4
Psalm 32:7	Psalm 18:1-2
Psalm 118:14	Psalm 91:2
Psalm 50:15	Psalm 36:5

 onfession. Following your time of praise, God may reveal some areas of your life that are not pleasing to Him. Take a few moments to **silently** confess those sins. Isaiah 59:2 tells us, *"But your iniquities have made a separation between you and your God, and your sins have hid His face from you so that He will not hear."* God says that He will not answer our prayer if there is unconfessed sin. Our relationship must not only be right with Him, but with our fellow man, if we desire Him to hear and answer our prayers.

How do we confess our sin when convicted by the Holy Spirit?
1. Name the sin specifically, agreeing with God that it is sin.
2. Repent concerning the sin. This will result in changed attitudes and actions.
3. Thank God that He has forgiven your sin because of what Christ did on the cross. I John 1:9 (King James): *"If we confess our sins, He is faithful and just to forgive us our sins and to cleanse us from all unrighteousness."*
4. Ask to be filled and controlled by the Holy Spirit. It is a matter of surrendering your will, a total commitment of yourself to God.
   - Command: Ephesians 5:18 (King James): *". . . but be filled with the Holy Spirit."*
   - Promise: I John 5:14-15 (NASB): *"And this is the confidence which we have before Him, that, if we ask anything according to His will, He hears us. And if we know that He hears us in whatever we ask, we know that we have the request which we have asked from Him."*
5. By faith, thank Him that He has filled you on the basis of His promise. Do not depend on your feelings. The promise of God's Word, not our feelings, is our authority.

hanksgiving. Another important aspect of a MITI meeting is in giving thanks for how God has answered our prayers. The Apostle Paul exhorts, *"In everything give thanks, for this is the will of God in Christ Jesus concerning you."* And in Psalm 50:23, God's Word tells us that when we give thanks we honor Him. *"He who offers a sacrifice of thanksgiving honors me."*

Instead of spending time telling the answer to your prayer, **pray** the answer. The other moms will join in one accord, thanking God with you.

First mom: "Dear Father, thank You that my son has found a Christian friend at school."

Second mom: "Thank You for perfect timing. You knew how lonely he was, and that he needed a Christian friend to help him be strong in You."

Third mom: "We thank You, Father, for Your goodness and that You truly care about every detail of his life."

When one subject is finished, another mom can introduce the next answer to prayer and so on.

Be sure to dedicate this time to thanksgiving only. It will be tempting to mention requests, but remember to focus on giving thanks.

ntercession. During this portion of our prayer time we come to God, interceding on behalf of our children, teachers and staff, school concerns and MITI. If your group is large, it would be best if you divide the ladies into smaller groups of two or three. The smaller group will allow more time to pray specifically for each child.

Children. The leader shares a Scripture verse to pray for the children. As we pray, placing our child's name in that passage, the power of God's Word drives out anxiety and fear and produces faith in us. Remember that faith is taking God at His word and acting accordingly. It is accepting God's words no matter what the circumstances, what the world says, or how we feel.

Here is an example of praying in one accord for our children using Colossians 1:10 (NIV). *"And we pray this in order that you may live a life worthy of the Lord and may please him in every way: bearing fruit in every good work, growing in the knowledge of God."*

First mom: "Dear Father, I ask that [Joe] would live a life worthy of the Lord and please [You] in every way, bearing fruit in every good work, growing in the knowledge of God..."

Second mom: "Yes, Father, I ask that [Joe] would conduct himself the way a Christian should, no matter how difficult the circumstances."

Third mom: "Oh Father, I agree with these prayers and ask that [Joe] would not live one way at home and church and another way at school. I ask that his Christian walk would be a part of every aspect of his life."

Second mom: "And, Father, that You would open his eyes to what really pleases You in his conduct."

You may continue praying for Joe on this subject, or be led to other thoughts in the verse. Be sure to exhaust all prayer thoughts for Joe before going on to the next child. Each child is prayed for using this Scripture verse.

After you have prayed Scripturally for each child, pray for the specific need of each child, such as a concern with a teacher, grades, for the salvation of friends, choice of friends, or communication at home. Be sure to record these requests.

Prayer Suggestions for our Children.

As you take one of the following Scriptures each week, you will begin to see the transforming power of God's word in your child's life.

Pray for their relationship with God:

- That they may know *"how wide and long and high and deep the love of Christ is, and know this love that surpasses knowledge"* (Ephesians 3:18,19)

- That at an early age they may accept Jesus Christ as their Savior (II Timothy 3:15)

- That they will allow God to work in their lives to accomplish His purpose for them (Philippians 2:13)

- That they will earnestly seek God and love to go to church (Psalm 63:1; Psalm 122:1)

- That they will be caught when guilty (Numbers 32:23)

Pray for godly attributes:

- That they will be protected from attitudes of inferiority or superiority (Genesis 1:27; Philippians 2:3)

- That they will respect authority (I Peter 2:13,14)
- That they will be the best students they can be (Colossians 3:23)
- That they will hate sin (Psalm 97:10)
- That they will be able to control their temper (Ephesians 4:26)
- That they will exhibit the fruit of the Spirit in their lives (Galatians 5:22)

Pray for relationships with family:

- That they will obey their parents in the Lord (Proverbs 1:8; Colossians 3:20)
- That they will accept discipline and profit from it (Proverbs 3:11,12; 23:13)
- That they will love their siblings and not allow rivalry to hinder lifelong positive relationships (Matthew 5:22; Ephesians 4:32)

Pray for relationships with friends:

- That unsaved friends will come to know Jesus (II Peter 3:9)
- That they will choose godly friends, who will build them up in the Lord, and be kept from harmful friendships that will lead them astray (Ecclesiastes 4:10; Proverbs 1:10)
- That they will be firm in their convictions and withstand peer pressure (Ephesians 4:14)
- That they will be a friend to the lonely, the discouraged, the lost (Matthew 25:40; Philippians 2:4)

Pray for protection:

- From the evil one (John 17:15)
- From drugs, alcohol, and tobacco (Proverbs 20:1; 23:31,32)
- From victimization and molestation (Luke 17:1,2)
- From premarital sex (I Corinthians 6:18-20)
- From physical danger—accidents and illnesses (Philippians 4:6)

Pray for their future:

- That they will be wise in their choice of a mate: pray now for the one who will marry your child, that he or she will be a Christian and remain pure, and that they will bring one another great joy (Proverbs 19:14)
- That they will be wise in the choice of a career (Proverbs 3:6)
- That they will be wise in the use of their God-given gifts, talents and abilities (Matthew 25:21)

God deals in miracles. There is nothing too hard for Him!

I Chronicles 28:9	Ephesians 4:1-2	James 4:8-9	I John 2:15-16
Colossians 1:9-11	Ephesians 4:23-25a	Deuteronomy 10:12-13	I John 3:7
Colossians 2:6-8	Ephesians 4:29	Romans 12:2	I John 1:8-9
Colossians 3:1-2	Philippians 3:10	II Timothy 2:15-16	Matthew 6:33
Ephesians 1:17-19	John 17:26	I Thessalonians 4:3-4, 7	Ephesians 5:1-3

Teachers/Staff. As we pray for teachers and staff, we can be confident that God is hearing and answering our prayers, even though we might not see the results.

It has been shared by many teachers how much they have appreciated and counted on our prayers. One teacher, with tears in her eyes, expressed how she couldn't believe that we would actually take the time and have the concern to pray for her. She thought that the only other person who ever prayed for her was her mom.

Begin by praying a specific Scripture for the teacher/staff:

Colossians 1:9-11	Ephesians 4:1-3	Philippians 3:10	II Timothy 2:24-25
Colossians 2:6-8	Ephesians 4:29	Colossians 3:12-15	I John 2:15-16
Ephesians 1:17-19	Ephesians 6:19-20	Colossians 3:17	I John 3:7
Ephesians 3:18-19	Philippians 1:9-11	Colossians 4:3-6	

Prayer Suggestions for Teachers:

1. That they will accept God's gift of salvation
2. That they will teach with excellence and creativity
3. That they will use speech that is gracious and pleasant
4. That they will consider each child as a special individual, not just as "their class" or "their job"
5. That they will have the zeal to make a difference for good in each student's life
6. That they will not grow weary in well doing, that their commitment to excellence and discipline will not wane
7. That substitute teachers will be able to control classrooms and be a welcome and positive influence
8. That those teachers going through difficult personal problems will seek God
9. That Christian teachers will recognize secular philosophies within the curriculum and openly stand firm in their values

Prayer Suggestions for Schools:

As we pray for school concerns, we release God's power to impact our child's school environment.

1. Pray that positions at the state and local level will be filled by men and women with godly principles and values.
2. Pray that new curriculum will be chosen wisely and that it will include biblical standards and high moral values.
3. Pray that each student will learn of God's great love and provision for salvation and accept God's forgiving grace.
4. Pray that children from difficult family situations will receive godly counsel, compassion from their teachers, and make healthy friendships.
5. Pray that your school will be drug and alcohol-free and no addictions will have hold on the youth.
6. Pray that God will protect students against unwise choices in extra-curricular activities.
7. Pray that there will be respect for one another, regardless of race or religion.

Prayer Suggestions for Moms In Touch International:

Please take a few minutes to pray for the ministry of Moms In Touch.

1. Pray for other moms to join your group.
2. Pray for each school (by name) in your district to have a MITI group.
3. Pray for a MITI group for every school in your city or immediate area.
4. Pray that every school in your state will have a MITI group.
5. Pray that every nation around the world will have moms praying for their children and schools.
6. Pray the Lord will give the MITI staff and board of directors wisdom and discernment in all decisions they must make on behalf of this ministry.
7. Pray that God will keep the MITI ministry pure and untarnished.

To facilitate following this format, a sample Member Sheet has been included on page 37. It may also be downloaded from the MITI website, www.MomsInTouch.org.

Praying for the Non-Believer

When someone's salvation seems impossible, we need to believe by faith Mark 10:27 *". . . with God all things are possible."* We are in a spiritual battle. But thank God that our spiritual weapons are mighty and our authority in Christ is far above the rulers, powers and forces of darkness. The enemy must yield (II Corinthians 10:3-5). We pray in the name of Jesus, asking for the salvation of students, teachers, and staff members. This takes faith, patience, and persistence. Remember, *"...greater is He that is in you, than he that is in the world."* (I John 4:4)

Here is an example of one accord praying for the non-believer:

First mom: "Dear Father, in the name of the Lord Jesus, I pray for the tearing down of all the works of Satan in the life of Pete."

Second mom: "I pray that his very thoughts will be brought into captivity to the obedience of Christ."

Third mom: "With the authority of the name of the Lord Jesus, I ask for Pete's deliverance from the power and persuasions of the evil one."

First mom: "I pray that his conscience will be convicted, and that You, God, will bring him to the point of repentance, and that Pete will listen and believe as he hears or reads the Word of God."

Third mom: "May Your perfect will and purposes be accomplished in and through Pete."

Here are some suggested Scriptures to study and incorporate in your prayer time for non-believers:

John 14:13	II Timothy 2:25,26
II Corinthians 4:3,4	I Timothy 2:4-6
II Peter 3:9	Romans 10:13-15
I Peter 1:18,19	Romans 5:8

Promises to Claim

Matthew 18:19-20 (NASB) *"Again I say to you, that if two of you agree on earth concerning anything that they may ask, it shall be done for them by My Father who is in heaven. For where two or three have gathered in My name, there I am in their midst."*

Luke 1:37 *"For with God nothing is ever impossible and no word from God shall be without power or impossible of fulfillment."*

John 14:13,14 *"And I will do—I Myself will grant whatever you may ask in My name (presenting all I Am) so that the Father may be glorified and extolled in (through) the Son. Yes, I will grant—will do for you—whatever you shall ask in My name."*

John 16:24 *"Up to this time, you have not asked a single thing in My name, but now ask and keep on asking and you will receive, so that your joy (gladness, delight) may be full and complete."*

James 1:5,6 (NASB) *"But if any of you lacks wisdom, let him ask of God, who gives to all men generously and without reproach, and it will be given to him. But let him ask in faith without any doubting, for the one who doubts is like the surf of the sea driven and tossed by the wind."*

I John 5:14-15 (NASB) *"And this is the confidence which we have before Him, that if we ask anything according to His will, He hears us. And if we know that He hears us in whatever we ask, we know that we have the requests which we have asked from Him."*

Psalm 84:11 (NASB) *"For the Lord God is a sun and shield; the Lord gives grace and glory; no good thing does He withhold from those who walk uprightly."*

I John 3:21-23 (NASB) *"Beloved, if our heart does not condemn us, we have confidence before God; and whatever we ask we receive from Him, because we keep His commandments and do the things that are pleasing in His sight. And this is His commandment, that we believe in the name of His Son Jesus Christ, and love one another, just as He commanded us."*

Hebrews 10:22,23 (NASB) *"Let us draw near with a sincere heart in full assurance of faith, having our hearts sprinkled clean from an evil conscience and our body washed with pure water . . . for He who promised is faithful."*

Luke 11:13 (NASB) *"If you then, being evil know how to give good gifts to your children, how much more shall your Heavenly Father give the Holy Spirit to those who ask Him?"*

Jeremiah 33:3 (NASB) *"Call to Me, and I will answer you, and I will tell you great and mighty things, which you do not know."*

John 15:7 *"If you live in Me—abide vitally united to Me—and My words remain in you and continue to live in your hearts, ask whatever you will and it shall be done for you."*

Matthew 21:22 *"And whatever you ask for in prayer, having faith and believing, you will receive."*

Words and Deeds

Words and Deeds is an **OPTIONAL** part of Moms in Touch

Once your group is well established and you choose to do Words and Deeds, a personal visit to your school principal is recommended.

Here are some suggested points to cover:
- Acknowledge your appreciation of the principal's leadership and the tremendous responsibility that he/she has.
- Share your concern for the pressures that young people are facing today.
- Let the principal know that you belong to a group of moms called Moms In Touch International who meet weekly to support the school through prayer.
- Indicate that your group of moms would like to bring treats at different times throughout the year to encourage and show appreciation to the faculty and staff.
- If a principal declines your offer, thank him/her graciously, present a card with your name and phone number, and ask him/her to call you if there ever is a time when the staff might benefit from some encouragement.

Encouragement Ideas for the School

Group. Several times throughout the year you may show appreciation to the entire staff by taking special treats. Be sure to include a card saying "We appreciate you," or something of a similar nature, and signed Moms In Touch International. Pray that these expressions of appreciation might reflect the love of the Lord. Here are some examples of what has been taken to schools: muffins, cupcakes, apples and nuts, cookies, basket of candies, sheet cake, donuts, fruit baskets, balloons, flowers, etc.*

More information is available in the Words & Deeds section of the MITI Leader's Guide

Your Moms In Touch group might plan a dessert, coffee or luncheon in order to express your appreciation in person. **Pray about everything, being sensitive to what might be appropriate for your school.** Instead of taking treats, one elementary MITI group wrote the following Christmas letter. It was so well received that we would like to share it with you. (If you choose to use this letter or another written encouragement for all teachers and staff, be sure to check with the school as to their procedures for distribution.)

Dear Teachers and Staff of .... ,
With the holiday season upon us, Moms In Touch International wishes each of you a wonderful season of celebration! And we thank you for the gifts you have given to us as mothers.

In September, we entrusted to you our greatest treasures—our children! Since that time, you have relentlessly and lovingly worked with them.

— You have given them the gift of self-esteem.
— You have given them smiles and approval when they achieved.
— You have given them hugs and understanding when they did not achieve.
— You have disciplined lovingly and fairly and earned their respect.
— You have persevered when our children have sometimes been less than pleasant to work with.
— You have recognized each child as a unique little person. You have striven to help each one begin to reach his or her potential.
Because you care, we know that your work does not always end at 3 p.m. every day. Perhaps you carry many of our little ones home with you occasionally—in your hearts.

So what can we offer you in return during this happy season of giving and receiving?

— We offer you our thanks for loving our children.
— We give you our support and encouragement.
— We offer our time when it is needed.
— We promise to pray for you . . . every week.
— We give you the "honor" of being the greatest elementary school staff anywhere.

Please accept these gifts. They are offered with much love and sincerity!

Moms In Touch International

Encouragement Ideas for the School

Group. Several times throughout the year you may show appreciation to the entire staff by taking special treats. Be sure to include a card saying "We appreciate you," or something of a similar nature, and signed Moms In Touch International. Pray that these expressions of appreciation might reflect the love of the Lord. Here are some examples of what has been taken to schools: muffins, cupcakes, apples and nuts, cookies, basket of candies, sheet cake, donuts, fruit baskets, balloons, flowers, etc.*

Your Moms In Touch group might plan a dessert, coffee or luncheon in order to express your appreciation in person.

Pray about everything, being sensitive to what might be appropriate for your school.

Instead of taking treats, one elementary MITI group wrote the following Christmas letter. It was so well received that we would like to share it with you. (If you choose to use this letter or another written encouragement for all teachers and staff, be sure to check with the school as to their procedures for distribution.)

Dear Teachers and Staff of .... ,
With the holiday season upon us, Moms In Touch International wishes each of you a wonderful season of celebration! And we thank you for the gifts you have given to us as mothers.

Statement of Faith

1. We believe the Bible to be inspired by the Holy Spirit, the only infallible, authoritative Word of God in all matters of faith and conduct.
   Deuteronomy 4:2; Psalm 19:7-9; Proverbs 30:5,6; I Corinthians 2:13; Galatians 1:8-9; II Timothy 3:15-17; II Peter 1:20-21; Revelation 22:18-19

2. We believe that there is one God, eternally existent in three persons: Father, Son, and Holy Spirit.
   Genesis 1:1-3; Isaiah 44:6-8; Matthew 28:19-20; Mark 12:29; John 1:1-4; Acts 5:3-4; II Corinthians 13:14

3. We believe in God the Father, an infinite, personal spirit; perfect in holiness, wisdom, power and love. We believe that He concerns Himself mercifully in the affairs of each person, that He hears and answers prayer, and that He saves from sin and death all who come to Him through Jesus Christ.
   Genesis 21:33; Isaiah 40:28; Exodus 33:14; John 4:24; Revelation 4:8; Romans 11:33-34; Jeremiah 32:17; Ephesians 1:19-20; Jeremiah 31:3; Romans 5:8; II Samuel 24:14; I John 5:14-15

4. We believe in God the Son, Jesus Christ the Savior, the only begotten Son of God, in His deity, in His virgin birth, in His sinless life, in His miracles, in His substitutionary and atoning death through His shed blood, in His bodily resurrection, in His ascension to the right hand of the Father, in His continuous intercession for His people, and in His personal return in power and in glory.
   John 1:1, 2, 14, 18; 3:16; Luke 1:34-35, 24:27; Hebrews 4:15; Romans 3:23-26, 8:34; Mark 8:38; Matthew 24:30; I Corinthians 15:3-4

5. We believe in God the Holy Spirit, the Helper and Comforter, in His daily guidance and revelation of truth, in His conviction of sin, righteousness and judgement, and in His indwelling presence at the moment of salvation, enabling believers to live godly lives.
John 3:5-8, 14:16-17, 16:13-14; Acts 1:8; I Corinthians 12:13; Ephesians 4:30-32, 5:18

6. We believe that everyone is born with a sinful nature, separated from God and in need of salvation. Regeneration by the Holy Spirit is absolutely essential for salvation through the repentance from sin and the acceptance of Jesus Christ as Lord and Savior.
John 3:5-8, 5:24; Ephesians 1:6-7, 2:8-9; Titus 3:5; I Peter 1:23; Acts 2:21

7. We believe in the resurrection of both the saved and the lost; the saved unto the resurrection of eternal life and the lost unto the resurrection of eternal damnation.
Luke 16:19-26; II Corinthians 5:8; Philippians 1:23; II Thessalonians 1:7-9; Revelation 20:11-15

8. We believe in the spiritual unity of believers in our Lord Jesus Christ.
Matthew 28:19; Acts 2:42-47; Romans 15:5-6; I Corinthians 11:23-26, 12:13

Policies

1. Any individual or group not adhering to the Moms In Touch International Statement of Faith or Policies shall not have the right to use the MITI name or logo, nor represent MITI in any manner.

2. Confidentiality brings integrity to the ministry; therefore, all prayer requests must be held in strictest confidence.

3. Moms In Touch International is not a lobbying group, regardless of how worthy the cause. Participation in outside political and social issues must be done solely on an individual basis. Under no circumstances should the MITI name be used in conjunction with outside issues.

4. Moms In Touch International prayer groups are not to hold their meetings on public school campuses.

5. Moms In Touch International prayer groups are not to solicit prayer requests nor place a prayer request box in any public school facility.

6. Moms In Touch International groups are not to use the public schools to promote the ministry, including advertisements or announcements in school newsletters. This includes handing out brochures to be sent home with the student body.

7. Unauthorized use of the Moms In Touch International name or logo is prohibited. It is the trademark of the MITI ministry, and its use requires the express written permission of the Moms In Touch International ministry.

8. Unauthorized sponsorship of speakers, Christian programs, videos, tapes, books, or any other outside materials or programs is prohibited without the express written permission of the Moms In Touch International ministry.

9. MITI rosters are for Moms In Touch use only. Under no circumstances are they to be loaned or shared with any other individual, organization or outside group. This includes personal use of the group roster to promote non-MITI events.

10. No form of advertisement may be placed inside or on any MITI booklet.

11. To allow for conversational prayer in one accord, moms who use other forms of prayer must refrain from them during the MITI hour; for example, speaking in tongues out loud or praying the rosary.

12. Moms In Touch International groups are not to engage in gossip or any conversation of a critical nature.

Guidelines

Each group is responsible to adhere to the **policies** of Moms In Touch International as they are **not optional**. It is **strongly recommended** that each group abide by the **guidelines**. They have been developed to provide the most powerful and effective use of the hour.

For Leaders

1. Read and re-read the Moms In Touch booklet to review the purpose, policies, and format.

2. Always begin and end the MITI hour ON TIME. You set the example.

3. Stress the importance of faithful commitment. Regular attendance will develop consistent prayer coverage as well as build trust, unity, and strength in the group.

4. Be responsible for registering the group by sending in the registration form. Update headquarters of any change in leadership.

5. Pray for and train a replacement, challenging the group members to not allow the group to disband.

6. Do not ask for testimonies, nor set levels of spiritual maturity for those who attend.

7. Encourage each member to have her own Moms In Touch booklet in order to be more informed as to how the group is to function. It is a wonderful resource for her own personal use.

8. Make sure that all members of the group receive a newsletter. Encourage each member of the group to sign up with MITI by mail or online www.MomsInTouch.org, to receive the MITI newsletter. This is a powerful tool to keep group members in touch with the world-wide ministry of MITI as well as keep them informed of upcoming events.

9. Coordinators and leaders who are also officers or active members in school organizations (PTA, site committees, etc.) are asked to pray and seek the Lord's wisdom in undertaking responsibility in both organizations. Great discretion is required to prevent a conflict of interest.

10. Provide the area coordinator or contact person with your name, address, phone number and school name, as well as that of the co-leader.

11. Attend the leaders meetings planned by the area coordinator. These meetings will provide encouragement, training, current ministry information and fellowship. If unable to attend, send a representative from your group.

12. If a leader has a concern or problem with a group member, she should speak with her privately, using a gracious and sensitive spirit.

13. If there is a problem or doubt about a situation, first contact the area coordinator. When necessary, the state coordinator or MITI headquarters are available to assist.

For Groups

1. Caution should be taken in terminology. Moms In Touch International groups pray *for* the schools, not *in* the schools. The misuse of one word may change the concept others have about the ministry.

2. The purpose of Moms In Touch International is to pray, not evangelize by sending gifts or messages with Scripture, Christian slogans, etc.

3. Words and Deeds is an *optional* activity of the Moms In Touch International group to show positive support to the school. It must not be a burden to the group financially or in time commitment. It is important for a group to be well established before the leader introduces MITI to the principal. Pray about the right time to make the contact. Where more than one group exists for one school, it is recommended that you coordinate the planned Words and Deeds activity.

4. Should a Moms In Touch member find it necessary to go to a teacher or principal concerning a child or a school-related matter, she is to go with a gracious spirit as a concerned parent without identifying herself as being part of Moms In Touch.

5. A mom who knows a teacher personally and is confident that the teacher is a Christian may ask for prayer requests privately. The name of a student should never be given by a teacher who may share a prayer request.

6. A Moms In Touch group prays for their *children* and matters that pertain to their *school*. Therefore, topics other than these must be prayed about before or after the MITI hour.

7. Moms with more than one child at the same school are encouraged to focus on *one child* each week. This allows for more concentrated and specific prayer for that child during the given time for intercession. Moms may alternate children weekly or focus on one child for several weeks or months.

8. Moms having children in two or more schools should ask the Lord to which school they should commit. Pray only for the child attending that specific school. A mom only commits to more than one MITI group if she will be faithful in her attendance to each group.

9. Each Moms In Touch group is to represent *one* school. The exceptions to this are where there are few students in wide geographic areas; college groups where several schools may be represented in one group; working moms; grandmother groups; church-based groups; and groups for special needs children.

10. When initially starting groups in an area, several schools may be represented in a combined group. This is to be a temporary situation because the longer the wait, the more difficult it becomes to separate. If there is only one mom for a school, it is acceptable for her to pray with another group until she has a prayer partner from her school. At that time they will form a new group.

11. Home schooling moms are encouraged to find others who are involved in home schooling and begin a Moms In Touch group.

12. A teacher whose own child attends the school is welcome to join the MITI group for that school.

13. Moms In Touch International prayer groups are specifically for women. Dads and parents who would like to pray for their children and school are encouraged to use the MITI format and materials.

14. If a mom has a specific prayer request for the school, she is to give it to the leader before the meeting. This will avoid unnecessary discussion during prayer time as well as give the leader opportunity to consider if it is appropriate for group time.

15. To avoid distractions during the MITI prayer hour, moms with pre-schoolers should allow another person the privilege of caring for her children.

16. Prayer-walking is an *optional* activity that must not take the place of the regular MITI hour. Walk around the school, not in or through the school. It must not be done during school hours.

Notes

Notes

MOMS IN TOUCH INTERNATIONAL
Member Sheet

Copy the Member Sheet for each member of your group. Start on time.
Materials needed: Bible, MITI booklet, pen

■ **Praise** – Praising God for **who He is**, His attributes, His name or His character. No answers to prayer or prayer requests during this time, please.

Attribute _____ Definition _____

Scripture(s) _____

_____

Thoughts: _____

_____

_____

■ **Confession** – Silent prayer time. Flows directly from praise time. Leader opens and closes this time of prayer.

■ **Thanksgiving** – Thanking God for answers to prayer, for things He has done. Flows directly from confession time. No prayer requests during this time, please.

_____

_____

_____

_____

_____

■ **Intercession** – Form groups of two or as comfortable.

■ **Intercession for Our Own Children** – Leader gives Scripture to pray for the week.

Child's Name _____ Scripture Request _____

_____

_____

Specific Request _____

_____

_____

Date/Answer _____

_____

■ **Intercession for Our Own Children** – *(continued)*

Child's Name _____ Scripture Request _____

_____

_____

Specific Request _____

_____

_____

Date/Answer _____ _____

_____

Child's Name _____ Scripture Request _____

_____

_____

Specific Request _____

_____

_____

Date/Answer _____ _____

_____

■ **Intercession for Teachers** – Leader gives each prayer group a faculty/staff person to pray for and a Scripture or topic for that week.

Teacher's Name(s) _____

Salvation Request *Open _____'s eyes and turn him/her from darkness to light, and from the power of Satan to God, so that he/she may receive forgiveness of sins and a place among those who are sanctified by faith. Acts 26:18*

Scripture or Topic _____

Specific Request _____

Date/Answer _____ _____

_____

■ **Intercession for School Concerns** _____

_____

Date/Answer _____ _____

_____

■ **Intercession for MITI** _____

_____

Date/Answer _____ _____

_____

Remember: What is prayed in the group, stays in the group!

ORDER FORM

To Insure Proper Processing
Print Clearly and Fill Out Completely

Name _____

Address _____

City, State, Zip _____

COUNTRY _____ Phone (_____) _____

E-mail Address _____

❑ I am a leader ❑ I need a mom to pray with
❑ I am a member other _____

School Name _____
❑ college ❑ high school ❑ middle school ❑ elementary ❑ home school

SchoolDistrict_____County_____

Comments

Item	Suggested Donation	Qty	Amount
English Booklet	$5.00		
*			
Words & Deeds Booklet	$2.50		
Leader's Guide (with binder)	$26.00		
Economy Leader's Guide (no binder)	$22.00		
Brochures ☐ *English* ☐ *Spanish*	Optional		
Promotional Video	$12.00		
Group Leader Training Video	$20.00		
Order Total			
20% Shipping within U.S.			
25% International Shipping			
Gift to Moms In Touch International (U.S. tax-deductible)			

☐ MC ☐ AMEX **Allow 3 - 4 weeks for delivery** TOTAL _____
☐ VISA
☐ Discover _____ EXP. _____

Signature _____

* OTHER BOOKLETS
$5.00 Arabic, Chinese, English UK, French, German, Italian, Korean, Portuguese, Romanian, Russian, Spanish, Swahili
$16.00 Braille

Make checks or money orders in U.S. currency payable to:
Moms In Touch International or MITI

Mail to: **MITI** or FAX to: **(858) 486-5132**
P.O. Box 1120
Poway, CA 92074-1120 U.S.A.

WEBSITE: www.MomsInTouch.org (On-line ordering available)

Thank you! We appreciate hearing from you and receiving your order.